HOME ON THE RANGE

Ranch-Style Riddles

by Diane and Andy Burns

pictures by Susan Slattery Burke

Lerner Publications Company · Minneapolis

To Nick and Donna Nicholson and Bill and Barb Goosman, dear western
*   friends. Keep your powder dry.* —D.L.B.
To my favorite Patrick McManus character, Rancid Crabtree —A.B.

To my wonderful daughter, Perrin, for her inspiration in this first year
*   of her life* —S.S.B.

This book is available in two editions:
Library binding by Lerner Publications Company
Soft cover by First Avenue Editions
241 First Avenue North
Minneapolis, MN 55401

Library of Congress Cataloging-in-Publication Data

Burns, Diane L.
  Home on the range : ranch-style riddles/by Diane and Andy
Burns ; pictures by Susan Slattery Burke.
     p.   cm. — (You must be joking!)
  Summary: A collection of riddles about ranch life and life out
West.
  ISBN 0-8225-2341-8
  1. Riddles, Juvenile. 2. Ranches—Juvenile humor. [1. Ranch
life—Wit and humor. 2. West (U.S.)—Wit and humor. 3. Riddles.
4. Jokes.] I. Burns, Andy. II. Burke, Susan Slattery, ill. III. Title.
IV. Series.
PN6371.5B864 1993
818'.5402—dc20   93-19158
                                                            CIP
                                                            AC
Manufactured in the United States of America

1 2 3 4 5 6 – I/JR – 99 98 97 96 95 94

Q: How does a rancher comb her hair?

A: With a sagebrush.

Q: How do you corral hiccuping ponies?
A: With burped-wire fences.

Q: How do mules open locked barns?
A: With don-keys.

Q: What kind of donkeys do you find underground?
A: Burrows.

Q: What do you call a sleepwalking horse?

A: A nightmare.

Q: How do mares wash their babies?

A: With saddle soap.

Q: What kind of sickness do wild horses catch?

A: Bronc-hitis.

Q: What do you call ground squirrels who run for exercise?

A: Prairie jogs.

Q: How are hibernating prairie dogs like bank robberies?

A: They are holed-ups.

Q: Where do shepherds invest their money?
A: In flocks and bonds.

Q: What do you call a swarm
of bees on the
prairie?
A: Hivestock.

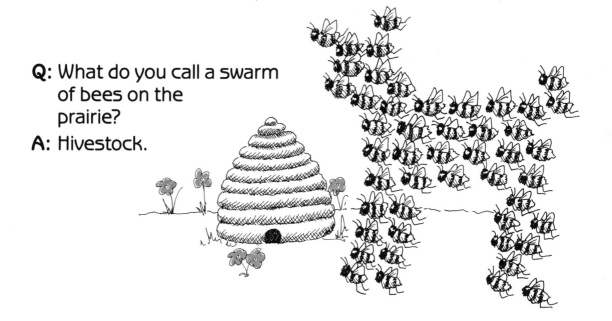

Q: Which streets lead to a roundup?
A: Roadeos.

Q: Where do outlaws live?
A: In the Bad-lands.

Q: Why are leaves in a high wind like outlaws?
A: They are rustlers.

Q: How do hens travel during a roundup?
A: In the chickwagon.

Q: Why did the rancher tiptoe through the pasture?
A: He had tenderfeet.

Q: What part of a rancher dries out the fastest?
A: His legs. They're always chapped.

Q: What happened to the rancher who fell into a haystack?

A: She baled out.

Q: What do you call a bull that tramps and wanders?
A: A bum steer.

Q: What do you call a dairy cow that won't be milked?
A: Udderly hopeless.

Q: What do you call cows and bulls when they're lying down?
A: Ground beef.

Q: How does a stallion purchase hay?
A: With his horse cents.

Q: Which ranch horse is the cheapest?
A: The quarterhorse.

Q: What spice grows on a ranch?
A: Sage-brush.

Q: What kind of food does a rancher cook
completely?
A: His thoroughbred.

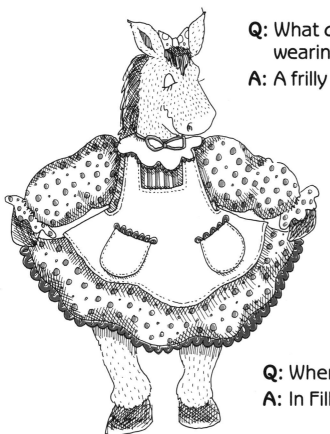

Q: What do you call a young horse wearing a fancy party dress?

A: A frilly filly.

Q: Which horse knows the alphabet?

A: The C-horse.

Q: Where are most ponies born?

A: In Filly-delphia.

Q: What is a horse's favorite food?

A: Pinto beans.

Q: Where do horses go on vacation?
A: Mare-land.

Q: What is a horse's favorite state?
A: Mane.

Q: What do you call stumbling bison?

A: Shuffleos.

Q: Where do buffaloes celebrate 200 years of history?

A: At their bison-tennial.

Q: How did the blacksmith get rid of a pesky pony?

A: He said, ''Horse, shoo!''

Q: How do ponies show that they're angry?

A: They leave in a hoof.

Q: What do you call runaway horses at dusk?

A: A stamp-eve.

Q: What did the runaway horse shout?

A: ''Whoa, whoa is me!''

Q: Which law officers live in swamps?
A: Marsh-alls.

Q: What do you call a law officer who falls into a watering trough?
A: The driputy sheriff.

Q: What expert ranchers are good at fishing?

A: Wr-anglers.

Q: What do you call wranglers who are always hungry?

A: Chowpokes.

Q: What do you call two cowpokes who meet for the first time?

A: Spurfect strangers.

Q: What do you call a horse if it never wins races?

A: An appaloser.

Q: What do ranchers put into pay telephones?

A: Quarterhorses.

Q: With what part of a tractor is a bull most familiar?

A: The steer-ing wheel.

Q: Why did the greenhorn put a bull on a tractor?

A: She wanted to see her cattle drive.

Q: What do you call the way a wrangler puts on her clothes?

A: Ranch-style dressing.

Q: What parts of a wrangler's gear are always unhappy?

A: His *sad*-dle and his *blue* jeans.

Q: How do ranchers get wrinkles out of their clothes?

A: With branding irons.

Q: What kind of weather will you find in a horse barn?
A: Rein-y.

Q: What street can be found in every horse corral?
A: Mane Street.

Q: In what part of New York City do wild horses live?
A: The Broncs.

Q: What kind of parties do horses like best?
A: Bridle showers.

Q: Where do cows hide their weapons?
A: In shoulder holsteins.

Q: What do you call pistols with the flu?
A: Sicks-guns.

Q: What do you call a grizzly on a stallion?
A: A bearback rider.

Q: How can you find a generic cow?
A: It's marked Brand X.

Q: Was the rancher hurt while sleeping in the pasture with his cattle?

A: No, the experience just grazed him.

Q: Why did the cowpoke sing a lullaby to a paper sack?

A: She needed a sleeping bag.

Q: Does a cowpoke ever get sick?

A: No, she just gets a little horse.

Q: What do you get when you cross a pasture with a barbed-wire fence?

A: Something that's haywire.

Q: What do you call happy dogs on the Oregon Trail?

A: A waggin' train.

Q: What patriotic song is a rancher's favorite?
A: "The Star-Wrangled Banner."

Q: What instruments do cattle play in an orchestra?
A: Long horns and short horns.

Q: What instruments do ranchers play?
A: Saddle horns.

Q: Why do ranchers make good pilots?
A: Because they're always on the Great Planes.

Q: What room in his house does a rancher like best?
A: The kitchen, because he's at home on the range.

ABOUT THE AUTHORS

Diane L. Burns, her son Andy, and their family have spent six summers as fire tower lookouts in Idaho's River-of-No-Return Wilderness. During the rest of the year they live in Wisconsin, where they manage a maple syrup sugarbush and dream of future trips out west. A former sixth grade teacher, Diane enjoys writing stories and talking with children. She and her cat, Rascal, spend their free time gardening. **Andy Burns,** a high school sophomore, reads and collects Patrick McManus and J. R. R. Tolkien novels. Happiest when he's out of school, Andy loves blacksmithing, wrestling, and rock climbing.

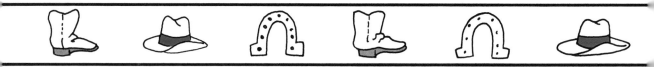

ABOUT THE ARTIST

Susan Slattery Burke loves to illustrate fun-loving characters, especially animals. To her, each of her characters has a personality all its own. She is most satisfied when the characters come to life for the reader as well. Susan lives in Minnetonka, Minnesota, with her husband, two daughters, and their dog and cat. Susan enjoys sculpting, reading, traveling, illustrating, and chasing her children around.

You Must Be Joking books

Alphabatty
Riddles from A to Z

Help Wanted
Riddles about Jobs

Here's to Ewe
Riddles about Sheep

Hide and Shriek
Riddles about Ghosts and Goblins

Ho Ho Ho!
Riddles about Santa Claus

Home on the Range
Ranch-Style Riddles

Hoop-La
Riddles about Basketball

I Toad You So
Riddles about Frogs and Toads

Off Base
Riddles about Baseball

On with the Show
Show Me Riddles

Out on a Limb
Riddles about Trees and Plants

Out to Dry
Riddles about Deserts

Summit Up
Riddles about Mountains

Take a Hike
Riddles about Football

That's for Shore
Riddles from the Beach

Weather or Not
Riddles for Rain and Shine

What's Gnu?
Riddles from the Zoo

Wing It!
Riddles about Birds